Divorce Wisdom

Smart Strategies for Anyone Contemplating or Experiencing Divorce

Juliet C. Laycoe

First published by Dog Ear Publishing
4011 Vincennes Road
Indianapolis, IN 46268
www.dogearpublishing.net

ISBN: 978-145756-660-8

This book is printed on acid-free paper.
Printed in the United States of America

Wisdom: the quality of having experience, knowledge, and good judgment; the quality of being wise.

–Google Dictionary

Contents

Introduction

In more than twenty years of practice as a family law attorney, I have experienced a lot of divorces. I have represented thousands of men and women, all with their own stories. I have represented the person who wants out of the marriage and the person who cannot let go of the marriage. I also have supported close friends and family members as they have gone through divorce. To say that divorce can be a difficult process is an understatement, whether you are a celebrity or an ordinary person. My profession requires me to work with people who are often at the very worst point of their lives. The emotions that are frequently present—such as anger, fear, grief, guilt, shock, and anxiety—are significant, and they impact not only the person who is going through the divorce, but also the divorce process itself.

My purpose in writing this book is to provide a general resource for people who are considering or experiencing marital separation or divorce. I include suggestions, examples, and opinions based on my own experiences, including actual divorce cases, consultations, seminars, and trainings. Names have been changed to maintain confidentiality. This book is not and should not be construed by any individual reader as legal or financial advice specific to the individual or the individual's circumstances.

I truly hope that the information and insights shared on these pages are helpful to you.

Chapter 1

Know What You Want

Sherri came to see me for an initial divorce consultation. Her mother accompanied her to the appointment and paid the fee. After sharing some introductory remarks and asking how I could help her, Sherri said that she wanted to get a divorce. She wanted to file the paperwork as soon as possible. I had noticed on the intake form that Sherri had been married less than one year, so I asked her what was going on, what caused her to be sitting in front of me that day. Sherri explained that she and her husband constantly argued. The arguments were explosive but not violent. They had not yet opened a joint bank account, and all their monthly bills were being paid out of Sherri's account. A few months into the marriage, her husband wanted a to buy new truck, but his credit wasn't very good. So, Sherri applied for the loan in

3

her name, and her husband got the truck he wanted. Sherri was paying for this truck out of her account, and she felt like her husband was sponging off of her. Sherri's mother nodded the entire time as her daughter spoke. Sherri was tearful and sad in our meeting. She said that she loved her husband, but she didn't like all the fighting and she knew marriage shouldn't be that way. When Sherri was finished, I asked her if they had ever talked about budgeting or how they would manage the household expenses before marriage. When she shook her head, I asked Sherri if she had told her husband that she was upset with their current arrangement for paying the bills. She shook her head again. I then asked if she had considered getting some help from a counselor on how she and her husband might better communicate with each other. Through more tears, Sherri said she was willing to go to counseling, but she was afraid to bring it up with her husband because he might say no.

Brandon and his wife had been married more than fifteen years and had three kids together. When he had an affair, Brandon and his wife agreed to separate, and he filed for divorce shortly thereafter. They already had been to court and had temporary court orders in place by the time Brandon ended up in my office. He retained my services to help him "finish up his divorce." In my third or fourth meeting with Brandon, he shared with me that he still loved his wife, that he regretted his affair and would choose to reconcile if she would agree. When I heard his feelings, I asked why he had filed for divorce if he still loved his wife and wanted to be married. He responded that he felt like he had no other choice but to file for divorce because his wife wouldn't talk to him after she discovered his infidelity.

Many people like Sherri and Brandon come to see me, uncertain as to whether or not they want a divorce. They still love their spouses, but they feel like they do not have options for their marriages. I always advise these people to be as sure as they can be about pursuing a course of action as permanent as divorce. Sometimes they are surprised by my advice and assume that I would always be pro-divorce because of my profession. Why would I advise people to consider marital reconciliation if I made my income from people getting divorced? The truth is, with the high rate of divorce in our society, I do not need help generating business. I am not pro-divorce. I am pro-happiness and fulfillment. I believe that marriages and relationships truly can add to our happiness and fulfillment. If a person is not sure whether he or she really wants to be divorced, it's worth the time it takes to examine their uncertainty before irreversible action is taken.

Of course, people do not always have a choice in the divorce process. If a person's spouse files for divorce and he or she really wants a divorce, the responding spouse doesn't have a choice; the choice is being made for him or her. In these cases, the spouse who has decided to end the marriage already has thought through the decision, and the other spouse often is playing catchup, grappling with his or her own understanding of why the marriage is over. The spouse who is left behind may be in denial, and the spouse who is leaving already may have moved out or moved on mentally or emotionally. Unfortunately, it is hard for a marriage to recover, if it had any chance to recover, after a spouse decides to divorce. In situations like the ones I have described above, however, the person *does* have a choice, and the marriage really *may* have a chance. In those cases, the question that should be examined is, "Are you sure?"

Ambivalence about divorcing or staying in a marriage is common. The decision to divorce is rarely an immediate one. Most of the time, people wrestle with their reasons and their emotions, swinging back and forth before making a final decision. Maybe an affair has occurred. Maybe a couple has already tried counseling, but nothing changed. Maybe one spouse feels bored in the relationship or not in love anymore. Regardless of the questions brewing in your mind, remember: *Divorce is permanent.* Infidelity is not necessarily fatal to a marriage. Marriages that experience infidelity can work through it. Marriage or couples counseling can be very helpful. Just as is the case with any other professional who provides a service, not all marriage counselors are created equal. Struggling couples need a counselor who is trained in marriage and family therapy. Successful marital therapy requires different skills and experience of a counselor than does individual therapy. For individuals or couples who are uncertain about divorcing or staying together, a specific type of counseling called *discernment counseling* may be very beneficial. Discernment counseling is not couples therapy. Discernment counseling is a process used to help spouses decide (or "discern") whether they want to end the marriage or pursue further counseling to work on their relationship.[1] The

---

1 More information on the discernment counseling process is available from various resources including The Doherty Relationship Institute (www.dohertyrelationshipinstitute.com).

process typically involves one to five sessions with a mental health professional. The couple meets both together and separately with the therapist. Through these meetings, the couple decides whether to 1) continue in the relationship as it is; 2) separate and divorce; or 3) commit to some kind of relationship therapy to work on their marriage. Couples who decide to pursue the third option are not necessarily deciding to stay in their marriage. Rather, they are deciding not to divorce right away while they attempt to make needed changes through therapy.

I encourage people like Sherri and Brandon to explore whether they really want to be divorced with a mental health professional on their own or participate with their spouse in discernment counseling. While it may be helpful for a person who is uncertain about the decision to divorce to talk through their reasons or emotions with a friend or family member, the person may not receive an objective ear or genuine assistance with the decision. The friend or family member hears only one side of the story and then forms and shares opinions that lack objectivity, because they care about the person and they want their loved one to feel better. The friend or family member is not concerned with objectivity. I suspected that Sherri's mother might have been pushing her into my office, so it was important for Sherri to examine her own feelings and questions. Sorting through whether your marriage is irreconcilable is an active task. I have held many consultations over the years with people who have been separated from their spouse for a very long time, yet they avoided taking any permanent action to resolve the status of their marriage. People hide behind the phrase "I am not sure," when the truth is that they doubt their own courage and strength to pursue a certain course of action, or they are fearful of their spouse's reaction or of the divorce process itself. Avoidance over the long term is not particularly helpful and does not promote happiness. Moreover, avoidance may increase unpleasant feelings such as regret or despair.

This was especially true for my client, Ron. He had been separated from his wife for approximately three years when he first arrived at my office for a consultation. It took him another year and a half to decide to file his petition for divorce. He was paralyzed with worry over his spouse's possible reaction and the financial consequences of a finalized divorce. One month after Ron filed for divorce, he was diagnosed with terminal cancer and given less than one year to live. Approximately three weeks after his final divorce decree was entered, Ron died. While I was glad that he had resolution to his marriage before he died, I felt such terrible sadness that Ron didn't have more time to experience contentment in his independent, post-divorce life.

Going through a divorce is not easy and may be very uncomfortable, but it is temporary. Life really is short—too short to avoid any temporary discomfort if the end game results in greater happiness and fulfillment for you. If you are contemplating divorce or marital reconciliation, make it an active process. If you are not comfortable speaking to or working with a mental health professional, seek out other reputable resources online or through articles, publications, and books. The following list may be helpful:

- *Should I Try to Work It Out?: A Guidebook for Individuals and Couples at the Crossroads of Divorce,* by Alan J. Hawkins, Ph.D., Tamara A. Fackrell, Ph.D. and J.D., and Steven M. Harris, Ph.D. and LMFT

- *The Divorce Remedy,* by Michelle Weiner Davis, MSW

- *To Divorce (or Not), A Guide, Part I: A Guide to Divorcing with Wisdom, Sanity and Integrity (Volume 1),* by Joseph Shaub, marriage and family therapist and attorney at law

- *After the Affair*, by Janice Spring Abrahams, Ph.D.

- *Take Back Your Marriage*, by William Doherty, Ph.D.

- *The 5 Love Languages*, by Gary Chapman

Finally, I need to address taking immediate action in cases of abuse or domestic violence. I am a strong proponent of making sure you want to be divorced before taking the step to end your marriage. However, if a person is being physically or emotionally abused by a spouse, I advocate for getting out of that situation first and then assessing the merits of reconciliation or divorce once you are removed from danger, or the threat of danger, and are safe. Equally important, if not more so, if you know or suspect that your spouse is abusing your child, your responsibility as a parent is to get your child out of that situation. Act first and evaluate later.

Bits of Wisdom

1. Divorce is a permanent course of action.

2. Be sure that you no longer want to be married before filing for divorce.

3. If you are uncertain whether you want to stay in your marriage, examine the question with a mental health professional.

4. In situations where abuse is occurring or suspected, remove yourself and your children from the situation first. Then, evaluate divorce or reconciliation.

Chapter 2

Get a Grip

Divorce is stressful. For some people, it may be the most stressful experience of their entire lives. Whether you are the person leaving the marriage or the person who was left, the circumstances generate all kinds of emotions— possibly intense and varied ones. Emotions, if not processed or handled with care, can wreak havoc in our lives, our children's lives, and our relationships with others. They can impact our ability to think clearly and act intelligently as we deal with stress.

Divorce triggers a wide range of emotions, including but not limited to sadness, anger, confusion, disappointment, frustration, fear, and guilt. Depending on how you address what is happening to you and how you are feeling while you are going through a divorce, your emotional

13

stability and your ability to participate meaningfully in the process may be compromised. The latter part of the foregoing sentence is very important: *Your ability to participate meaningfully in the process may be compromised.* You may have read that sentence and determined that you do not need to participate, because you do not want to be divorced. Or you may have dismissed the sentence entirely, because you just want out of your marriage and do not care what happens in the process or what you have left when it is finished. *Pause.* Divorce, while an important life event, is not a *single* event. The effects of a divorce—psychological, financial, and legal—continue long after a judge has signed the final judgment or decree. So, getting a grip on your emotions sooner rather than later in the divorce process can be critical to your overall well-being, both in the present and in the future.

Marcy and her husband were married for nine years when he went overseas for employment. While working overseas, he had multiple affairs, a fact he did little to conceal from Marcy. She was devastated. She had married later in life at the age of forty-four, and she'd coveted the status of being someone's wife. She did not want to be divorced. When it was clear that her husband had no intention of returning to the States or putting a halt to his extramarital escapades, Marcy reacted with a vengeance. She retained me to help her file for a legal separation and obtain a temporary spousal support order. When I filed a petition with the court on her behalf, I did not know that she had already liquidated their joint bank accounts, changed the logins and passwords to all their financial accounts, and eliminated her husband's access to jointly held credit cards. She got rid of her husband's personal belongings at their house and threatened the people she believed were having affairs with him. Marcy's behavior made it very difficult for me to be an advocate for her. Just when I thought one fire had been put out, her husband's attorney would notify me of another fire Marcy had set. Valuable time was wasted, and greater attorney fees were incurred trying to extinguish the flames.

Marcy's intense emotions wouldn't allow her to hear or accept the information and legal counsel I was trying to provide to her. She did not trust me—she did not really trust anyone. Her anger and rage eventually subsided, and she sank into a deep depression. At one point, she was admitted to the emergency room for suicidal ideations. A short time later, Marcy and I ended our professional relationship. She needed more help than I could provide. Until she tended to her mental health,

Marcy would not be able to participate meaningfully or responsibly in the legal process, not even with an attorney representing her.

John and his wife had been separated for several years before he landed in my office. His wife had already filed for divorce. They had tried to resolve the issues in their divorce outside of a court process but were unsuccessful. John was despondent and refused to accept that they would need a judge to decide their case for them. He had worked as the office manager in their business but had quit or was terminated when his wife moved out of their home. John didn't believe that he would be able to get another job because of his age. His wife still worked in the business and earned a substantial paycheck, and the business paid for several of her personal expenses. John did not want any more conflict, so rather than ask for financial support from his wife or access to their joint funds, he crept along each month on the income he received from Social Security.

John's fear of conflict and sense of despair adversely impacted my representation of him. He was intelligent but often interpreted case-related questions that I presented to him as personal attacks, and time normally spent between attorney and client on strategy was derailed. While he was respectful to me, John did not always follow my recommendations on what was necessary and important to prepare his case for trial. Unfortunately, this stubbornness likely cost John tens of thousands of dollars. I could not get him to agree to hire an outside professional to value a specific asset that would be distributed in the divorce. His wife ended up with the asset at a value John strongly felt was unfair, but the judge had limited evidence to support any other result.

As a divorce attorney, I work with people who are immersed in unpleasant and painful situations. I see ordinary, good people at their worst. Sometimes these ordinary, good people do dumb things or make bad choices during their divorce process. Other times, people are so paralyzed by their own emotions that they cannot make necessary decisions, advocate for themselves, or, in John's case, aid their attorney in representing them. The intense emotions experienced during divorce can cause people to act out of character. People can be tempted to seek vengeance or behave badly when they are hurt by or angry with someone they had loved and trusted so very much. Yet, behaving badly, being unreasonable, or acting vengefully in a divorce process has numerous consequences.

A person who behaves badly, acts unreasonably, or is spiteful during a divorce typically pays more in attorney fees. Attorney fees are incurred every time an attorney deals with the fallout of bad behavior, like I did every time I was contacted by the attorney of Marcy's husband about something she had done. In some instances, a judge may order the person who is behaving badly or acting unreasonably to pay their spouse's attorney fees as well as their own. Unlike the chewing gum commercial from years ago, double attorney fees are not double the fun.

Bad behavior is frowned upon by judges and others involved in a divorce proceeding. If a judge is issuing decisions in a divorce, or if another professional such as a parenting or custody evaluator is providing recommendations in a divorce case, a person's truthfulness and credibility may be questioned when he or she is behaving poorly or acting out. Remember that decisions made in a divorce can impact you for a lifetime. You do not want the individuals with decision-making power or influence in a divorce proceeding to be distracted by bad behavior. Moreover, a person going through a divorce must maintain a grip on their own emotions so that he or she can make intelligent decisions about the future. If you cannot make decisions due to your own grief or emotional paralysis, or if you cannot control your own bad behavior, the divorce process may be delayed. And delays in a divorce proceeding mean that attorneys are being paid longer, and closure—emotional or otherwise—cannot occur.

A divorce proceeding takes time and involves two primary people—the couple who is uncoupling. Regardless of whether or not you are the person who wants out of the marriage, be mindful of your actions, and pay attention to the feelings of your spouse. Your spouse's willingness to participate in the divorce process, let alone strike a settlement agreement with you, may be wrecked if you are outwardly making plans for a new single life and flaunting a new beau at your son's soccer game. Updating your status to "single" on your social media accounts and posting pictures from the cruise you had planned to take with your spouse months ago but decided to take your girlfriend on instead is a recipe for some amount of trouble. I am, of course, not saying that you are responsible for what your spouse does, thinks, or feels. But I am saying that your actions *do* impact your spouse and the divorce process. Be conscientious. Cool your jets, and for Pete's sake, don't bring your new girlfriend or boyfriend to meetings with your attorney, your spouse, your spouse's attorney, or any settlement or court proceedings. It's incredibly poor form, and likely, the girlfriend or boyfriend has nothing so valuable to add to the process that would offset the adverse consequences.

Getting a grip on your emotions during a divorce means different things for different people. Counseling is helpful for some people, while other people benefit from therapy or support groups. Do not minimize your need for help. Divorce is stressful and often traumatic. While you may believe you are okay, you are not invincible, and you don't have to act that way. The divorce process can be an emotional roller coaster, and the following suggestions may be helpful if your ride is bumpy:

- Find a mental health professional at the outset of your divorce and get a mental health checkup. Maybe you decide one therapy appointment is all you need, but you will have a resource available for you in the future if you need one.

- Participate in regular counseling sessions. The structure of ongoing mental health support may be very beneficial even if it's for a temporary duration.

- Get a divorce coach. A divorce coach is a mental health professional, but the service provided is not therapy. Coaching focuses on future improvement, while therapy often focuses on healing from the past or treating a mental health diagnosis or behavior. A divorce coach educates and supports people going through a divorce and helps them work through emotional barriers that may hinder the ability to reach a settlement and/or participate in the divorce process.

- Schedule an appointment with your primary care physician, and be open to suggestions provided for handling stress, coping with grief, and managing your emotions.

- Join a divorce support group; many counselors, churches, and hospitals offer them.

- Try not to download your emotions onto your attorney. Although divorce attorneys may be used to clients' intense and varied emotions, most attorneys are not trained mental health professionals and they shouldn't be used as such. Attorneys should be paid only for the services they are licensed to provide for their clients.

Bits of Wisdom

1. The intense emotions felt during a divorce can impact the divorce process.

2. Getting a grip on your emotions will help you think clearly, act rationally and make reasoned decisions about your life and the lives of your children.

3. Be conscientious about what your spouse may be feeling or how your spouse might react to your words or actions during the divorce process.

4. Do not be afraid to seek professional help and support even if doing so is limited to one appointment or a few sessions.

5. Divorce is not a single event. The effects of a divorce last long after a final judgment is entered with a court.

Chapter 3

Find an Attorney and Assemble Your Team

Divorce can seem isolating and scary. You may feel alone, discouraged or completely out of control of your own future. Assembling a team of professionals to assist and guide you and be a resource to you is incredibly helpful as you are chartering the rough waters of a divorce. The professional players on your team may vary depending upon your circumstances, but it is important to choose the players thoughtfully for their knowledge and expertise.

Your team roster should include the following players:

1. Attorney

Gaining a better understanding of the divorce process and the laws and options for your circumstances from an attorney can be a great comfort during a time of so much uncertainty. I strongly recommend that you consult with an attorney at least once to review your situation and obtain relevant advice. You don't want to consult with just any attorney. Talking with the uncle of your cousin's boyfriend who practices criminal defense in another state is not going to be particularly helpful for you. While the uncle may have good intentions, he is not proficient in family law and does not know the laws or the process in your state. You should consult with an attorney who specializes in family law and practices law in the state where your divorce will occur. Because local court rules and procedures can differ among counties in your state, you may want to consult with an attorney in the county where your divorce will occur. Regardless of whether you ultimately decide to retain the services of an attorney to help you with your entire divorce process, at least sit down once for a consultation with a family law attorney.

How do you find an attorney? While you can search online for family law or divorce attorneys in your area, you should ask for referrals from friends, colleagues, and other people you know who have used the services of an attorney. Sometimes the referral is made directly to a divorce attorney. Other times the referral may be directed to an attorney who specializes in another area of the law but who can provide you with names of well-regarded divorce and family law attorneys in your area. After you have the referrals in hand, check out the bios and background information on each attorney's website. Be aware that online reviews or rating scores can be misleading, as some attorneys pay a fee for a higher score or prominent presence, and a poor online review or rating may not be a true representation of the attorney's performance or work. Similarly, an attorney's high rating and flashy website does not mean that he or she is a rock star divorce magician. Again, asking friends or people you know about their experiences with an attorney may be the most valuable strategy for you as you are trying to find an attorney.

How do you know if an attorney is a good fit? First and foremost, take the time to interview potential attorneys by scheduling an initial consultation. You should feel comfortable with the attorney and believe that you will be able to share information openly and honestly with the attorney.

Attorneys perform their job the best when they have adequate and truthful information available from a client. Feeling comfortable and confident in the attorney you choose to represent you may mean that you meet with two or more attorneys for initial consultations. It's like comparison shopping. Experience what an attorney is like and how you feel about that person when you are sitting across from them at a table or a desk. Do not just rely on your best friend's experience. While your best friend may have loved her attorney, the same person may not be a good fit for you. Trust your own perception and comfort level.

What else should you consider when selecting an attorney? Many important considerations should guide you when you are selecting an attorney.

- *The attorney should charge for the initial consultation.* You should receive substantive information from an initial consultation. A fee is appropriate when you receive something of value from a professional. Expecting free advice is not reasonable, and attorneys who offer a "free consultation" may not be providing you with substantive or relevant information for your situation. Some lawyers charge a flat fee for an initial meeting while others charge an hourly rate. Make sure you are aware of the fee when you schedule the consultation.

- *Is the attorney listening to you or downloading information?* The attorney should be doing both—listening to you and providing you with relevant information. While the attorney may handle divorce cases routinely, each case and set of circumstances is different. The attorney should be listening to your concerns and taking the time to answer your questions throughout your consultation or case.

- *Does the attorney explain the fees and billing procedures?* As noted above, you should be aware of the initial consultation fee before you even arrive for the first appointment. Likewise, you should walk away from the initial consultation with an understanding of what the monetary requirements will be if you decide to retain an attorney to assist you with your entire divorce process. After the initial consultation, you should know the hourly rates for the attorney and any support staff in the firm who will be working on your matter. Most attorneys require a retainer or fee deposit, which is an up-front monetary deposit that you pay to the attorney to engage him or her in providing professional services. Retainers and fee deposits can vary depending upon the complexity of your case. Some attorneys may have a standard fee deposit or retainer for all clients. Other attorneys may prefer to discuss the fee deposit or retainer with you after they learn more about your circumstances in the initial consultation and determine the professional services that will be necessary. In addition to the retainer or fee deposit, you may be required to pay for professional services provided to you at regular or monthly intervals. All monetary requirements, billing procedures, and details regarding hourly rates and costs you will be expected to pay should be set forth in a written fee, engagement, or professional services agreement that you sign at the beginning of your attorney/client relationship.

- *Make sure you know what to expect if you hire the attorney.* The attorney should be able to tell you during the initial consultation what you can expect if you retain (i.e., hire) him or her. If the attorney has staff, you should know who they are, what duties they perform, and how the attorney uses them. You should understand how best to communicate with the attorney, whether that is by phone, e-mail, text message, or through the attorney's assistant. You also should know the attorney's usual response time when you do you contact him or her. Do not be offended if the attorney instructs you to contact his or her support staff with questions or concerns. Support staff often can provide quicker responses and/or relay information to and from the attorney if he or she is tied up in appointments or court. Finally, make sure you know what professional services will be provided to you in the immediate future and if there is any information or documentation the attorney needs in order to provide those services.

- *The attorney should explain options, laws, and other relevant information in a way you understand.* An attorney should speak to you clearly and not flood the conversation with legal terms that you do not know and which the attorney does not explain. Remember that you may have a long-term relationship with your attorney. If you can't understand what he or she is saying during the initial consultation, or if you do not care for the way he or she is speaking to you, it may be a sign that this attorney is not a good fit for you.

- *The attorney/client relationship should be reciprocal.* When you hire an attorney, the professional relationship is a two-way street. You should not expect that hiring an attorney means that he or she will handle everything without your involvement. Be wary if an attorney tells you otherwise. You must be a participant in the process. This is your life. The outcome of decisions made during your divorce affects you, not your attorney. You need to provide complete and accurate information to the attorney. In turn, the attorney educates you on the laws, processes, and options available to you so that you can make informed decisions.

- *It is okay to get a second opinion.* Some of the decisions made during your divorce process may have a lifetime impact. You should rely upon your attorney's advice and expertise when considering possible options and scenarios. If you really are struggling with a decision or are concerned about a strategy or course of action suggested by your attorney, consider scheduling a consultation with a different attorney for a second opinion. Sometimes the perspective from a different attorney may help you assess options or feel comfortable with a decision in your divorce process. However, use the second opinion consultation objectively and sparingly; do not obtain a second opinion just because you do not like what your attorney has shared with you. Attorneys cannot always deliver good news, and the reality that attorneys sometimes have to share with clients can be a tough pill to swallow. You also should not routinely consult with a different attorney because you are uncomfortable with the advice and recommendations provided to you by the attorney you chose to retain. Doing so may be an indication of a bigger problem—that you do not trust your attorney or feel confident in your attorney's expertise. To solve this problem, you may need to retain a different attorney to represent you. I once consulted half a dozen times with a person represented by a prominent local divorce attorney. After the third or fourth consultation, I concluded that this person had lost confidence in his attorney's advice. Yet he was afraid to break off the relationship with his attorney. He even contacted me from a mediation session being conducted with his attorney and his wife and her attorney. Changing attorneys is not uncommon. If you aren't comfortable in the professional relationship you have with your attorney, know that it is okay to switch horses, but you cannot ride two horses at one time. Be mindful that consistently second-guessing your attorney's advice or declining your attorney's recommendations can create conflict in the professional relationship, which your attorney may then terminate.

2. Accountant

When you divorce, the assets and debts you own with your spouse are divided in some way. You may decide to sell your home. As part of the settlement, you may split a brokerage account with your spouse, liquidate or partially liquidate an investment or withdraw funds from a retirement account to pay off debt. If you have children, you must decide where they will live. You may pay or receive child support, spousal support, or post-secondary educational support. These actions may have tax implications, some good and some not good. Additionally, when you divorce, how you file your income tax return or who prepares it may change, and the amount you owe for federal or state income taxes may be different. I highly suggest receiving guidance from an accountant regarding potential tax consequences or benefits of certain actions and decisions made during and after your divorce process. If you do not know an accountant or currently use one, ask for a referral from your attorney, friends, or family members.

3. Financial Advisor

Financial advisors are experts in personal finance. They offer expertise in financial and retirement planning to help you make the most of your income and financial resources. When you work with a financial advisor, you gain a better understanding of your finances, and you receive support for establishing your financial goals both in the short term and in the long term. A divorce can create many changes in your finances and financial plans. Instead of using a couple's available income to support one household and save for retirement, two households, each with their own monthly expenses, are established in a divorce. You may not be familiar with budgeting because you relied on your spouse to manage these tasks during your marriage. If you were relying upon your spouse's retirement account or pension as part of your retirement plan, you may need a new plan for retirement once you are divorced. You may lack the financial acumen to determine how to invest any assets you receive as part of your divorce award. You may not know how to equitably split securities (i.e., stocks and bonds) with your spouse so that you each end up with a properly balanced portfolio after the divorce. A financial advisor provides support and guidance for all these scenarios. A financial advisor can help you feel more educated about your current financial circumstances and more confident in planning for your future. You should consider meeting with a financial advisor early in your divorce process.

4. Insurance Professional

Divorcing and creating two separate households requires you to change insurance policies for health, auto, life, or home ownership at some point. You cannot maintain a joint automobile insurance policy with your former spouse. If you are covered under your spouse's health insurance plan, you need to secure your own coverage after divorce. If you have life insurance, you may be considering whether to keep the policy and expense of the premium after your divorce. You may be required to maintain a life insurance policy to secure your court-ordered support obligations. You could decide to purchase a home of your own after you divorce; if so, you will need a homeowner's insurance policy. While you can get quotes online or use different companies for each type of insurance, talking to an insurance professional who can assist you with all of your various needs might be beneficial. Sometimes you will pay less in premiums for bundled policies. And sometimes you need to have the coverage details explained to you in plain words. Do not be afraid to ask questions, obtain comparable quotes for coverage, or talk to several different insurance professionals. Ask for referrals for insurance professionals from friends, family members, or other people you trust.

5. Real Estate Professional

A real estate professional is more than just someone who sells homes. In the divorce process, a real estate professional can help you determine the market value of your home and estimate what you will receive in proceeds after closing costs and mortgages are paid, as well as how long it may take for your home to sell based on the current state of the housing market. Many real estate professionals will provide you with a summary of comparable sales in your area at no charge. If you plan to purchase another home after your marital home is sold or your divorce is final, the same real estate professional should be able to assist you in lining up closing dates, and they may be able to offer you a reduced fee for handling two sales transactions. You should make sure that the real estate professional you choose is comfortable working with people who are divorcing and who may not be completely agreeable with each other at times. If you are concerned that you owe more on your house than what it may be worth, hire a real estate professional with experience handling short sales. A short sale is a *sale* of real estate in which the net proceeds from selling the property will fall *short* of the debts secured by liens against the property.

6. Mental Health Professional

In chapter 2, I discussed the importance of connecting with a mental health professional throughout the divorce process. Therapy can be critical to your emotional recovery from a divorce. Therapy also can be extremely helpful for children who are struggling with their parents' separation. Individual therapy is not the only service provided by mental health professionals. Depending upon your circumstances, you may consider using a mental health professional for the following:

- *Divorce coaching:* a flexible, goal-oriented process designed to support, motivate, and guide people going through divorce to help them make the best possible decisions for their future, based on their interests, needs, and concerns.

- *Parent coaching:* a process that helps parents with parenting challenges by developing strategies to shift behavior and thinking and offering alternative perspectives around family situations.

- *Co-Parenting Counseling:* a process that provides parents with the tools they need to improve how they communicate about their children and establish boundaries for a better long-term co-parenting relationship with each other.

- *Support groups:* groups designed to assist individuals, parents, and children who are coping with difficult emotions related to divorce or separation.

7. Friends and Family Members

You may be ending a love relationship, but you still have people in your life who love and care for you. Spend time with friends and family members who can provide additional support to you and hopefully interject some fun into your life during this difficult time.

In closing this chapter, I am reminded of the proverb, "It takes a village to raise a child." Similarly, I believe we all need the support of a village—a group of trusted people who are willing and able to help us plan, process, and achieve our goals in a safe environment. And at no time is this more important than when you are facing a traumatic life event such as a divorce.

Bits of Wisdom

1. Information and advice from professionals with different areas of expertise can be very helpful to you during the divorce process.

2. Consult with an attorney who specializes in family law in the state where you will be divorced to review your situation and obtain relevant advice.

3. If you do not know any attorneys, ask for referrals from friends, colleagues, and other people you know who have used the services of an attorney.

4. Consider consulting with other professionals such as an accountant, financial advisor or insurance professional to review your circumstances and plan.

5. Therapy and other services provided by mental health professionals can support your emotional stability and recovery throughout your divorce.

Chapter 4

Prepare Yourself

Joan had been married for nearly thirty years. Her husband had become involved with another woman and wanted to leave the marriage. Joan never had contemplated that her marriage would end, but her husband certainly had anticipated it. She came to our consultation with a piece of paper that her husband had given to her. The paper included a handwritten list of their assets and debts, with dollar values and balances cited, as well as her husband's notations on how he believed everything should be divided. I asked Joan what she thought about the list and whether the listing of assets and debts was accurate. She could not answer with certainty. I gently pressed Joan to explain why she felt uncertain. She told me that she knew they owed money on their house and had bank and retirement accounts, but she knew nothing specific or independent beyond what her husband had put on the handwritten list. Her husband had managed every aspect of their finances throughout their marriage. She shared with me that he would tell her what account to use for withdrawing money when she needed cash and which credit cards to use for certain purchases. He regularly provided her with new cards from different credit card companies and further instructions on how she should use them. He obtained loans and credit cards sometimes without her knowledge and sometimes in her name without her knowledge. Joan told me about the last refinance they had completed on their home mortgage. She thought the purpose of the refinance was to get a better interest rate on the loan and use some of their equity to pay for a modest home repair. She was shocked to see more than $60,000 in consumer credit card debt listed on the closing statement for the new loan. This debt was paid off as part of the refinance, but Joan felt sick that the equity they had built in their home over the years was gone. She was defensive and upset that she had trusted her husband. She had grave concerns that more debt would surface, and she was extremely suspicious that her husband had hidden assets somewhere.

In my practice, I have worked with many people in circumstances similar to Joan's, who depend completely on their spouse to manage the household finances and who consequently are unfamiliar with their assets, debts, and monthly expenses. While it isn't uncommon for spouses to have different duties in a marriage, I've observed that the allocation of those duties can create disadvantage and the escalation of fear if a divorce takes place. In Joan's case, a considerable amount of time was spent gathering information and documentation to construct a picture of the couple's assets and debts. Joan's lack of confidence in her own knowledge and trust in her husband caused us to put more effort into tracing where all their money went. Even with thousands of pages of bank records, credit card statements, and other documents, Joan still felt very insecure during the settlement negotiations.

Being comfortable in your knowledge of your financial circumstances and having independent and reliable information about your assets, expenses, and debts minimizes risk during a divorce. You need to avoid making an uninformed, uneducated, or premature decision that impacts you, your children, and your future for years to come. The risk of this happening can be mitigated, however, and here are some ways to do it:

1) Prepare and educate yourself.

Divorce causes inevitable change. One household becomes two. Monthly expenses are managed in different ways. Shared assets are divided. Support obligations may be established that require each spouse to reprioritize the budget or reallocate their income. A clear understanding of your financial circumstances at the onset of a separation or divorce is essential.

If you are unfamiliar with your own finances, **start learning what income you receive and what you spend each month.** How? **Review your bank statements.** If you do not have paper statements or know how to access your account online, contact your bank to set up online access or ask them to provide you with statements for the past six to twelve months. Six to twelve months should get you started, and you can review the statements further back if necessary. Do the same with your credit card statements. Investigate any expense, charge, or withdrawal that you do not recognize.

Gather and study your tax returns, your retirement and investment statements, and your property tax and/or home mortgage statements. Expect your attorney to ask you for those statements at some point in the divorce process. Gathering the statements now and becoming acquainted with the content can be helpful to both you and your attorney. If none of these statements exists in your home and you do not feel comfortable asking your spouse where to locate them, contact the accountant or tax preparation specialist who assisted with your tax returns and request copies. Ask for statements or account summaries from your mortgage lender. If you do not know who your mortgage lender is, look at your bank statement and find the mortgage payment transaction, listed either as a debit or a cancelled check. Note that you might not be able to obtain statements on any retirement, investment, or financial accounts in your spouse's sole name without your attorney's involvement. If you know the firm managing the accounts, however, you might be able to obtain some information or specific figures on any accounts that are also in your name.

Obtain a credit report for yourself. Whether you have access to your credit card statements or not, requesting a recent credit report is useful. The federal Fair Credit Reporting Act requires the three nationwide credit reporting companies—Equifax, Experian, and TransUnion—to provide you with a free credit report every twelve months. You can order your credit report by visiting www.annualcreditreport.

com. A credit report shows any current and past debt obligations associated with your name and Social Security number. If you do not recognize any of the creditors or debts listed on your report, you should contact the creditor directly for more information. Because the debt is associated with your name and Social Security number, you should have access to the account history. You can dispute any inaccuracies through the credit reporting company. Step-by-step instructions for submitting a dispute can be found on the Federal Trade Commission's consumer pages at www.consumer.ftc.gov.

Identify any open credit card accounts held in both your name and your spouse's name. Having a jointly held credit card with your spouse means that either one of you can use it. Sometimes people in the turmoil of a divorce are not responsible with their use of credit. Do not be surprised by a pile of debt associated with your name and Social Security number on a joint credit card. If you do not have an outstanding balance on a joint credit card, you should be able to close out the account. Note that the credit card company may require your spouse's consent. If you cannot obtain your spouse's consent or if you have an outstanding balance, ask the credit card company to freeze the account, which means that neither you nor your spouse will be able to use the card for further purchases. You also may request a temporary restraining order prohibiting either you or your spouse from incurring joint debt in the legal divorce process. A final note to keep in mind as it relates to joint credit card accounts: Even if your spouse agrees to pay the credit card or a court order requires him or her to do so, you are not absolved of the liability as far as the credit card company is concerned. Your name and Social Security number still are associated with the credit card obligation. If your spouse does not pay the credit card balances, your credit can be impacted adversely, and the credit card company may look to you for payment.

Obtain a credit card solely in your name. Jointly held credit cards may be closed or frozen in the divorce process either with or without your knowledge. A restraining order may be ordered by the court that prohibits you from using a joint credit card. If access to joint funds has been circumvented for whatever reason during your separation or divorce, you may need to use credit to pay for daily needs, emergency expenses, or attorney fees. A separate credit card also may provide you with some autonomy in how you choose to spend your money.

Know what type of insurance policies you have in place and what you will no longer have in place

after your divorce. Do you have health, dental, or vision insurance? Auto insurance? Life insurance? Become familiar with the existing benefits that you have under each plan and consider any needs that should be addressed sooner rather than later. Are you putting off a specific medical or dental procedure? If so, you may want to get it done before you change coverage. Also, find out if your health insurance policy covers mental health therapy or counseling. Do not be afraid to use the mental health benefit for yourself or your children during the divorce process. If you lose your spouse's employment-related health insurance because of a divorce, you may be offered COBRA coverage. The Consolidated Omnibus Budget Reconciliation Act (COBRA) gives employees and family members who lose their health benefits the right to choose to continue group health benefits provided by their group health plan for limited periods of time under certain life event circumstances, such as job loss, death, or divorce. While you may be able to continue coverage under COBRA, you still must pay the premium for the continued coverage, which is often more expensive than securing independent health insurance.

For life insurance policies, do you know whether the policy has a cash surrender value? The cash surrender value is the sum of money an insurance company pays to a policyholder if the policy is voluntarily terminated before its maturity or if an insured event occurs; this is often considered an asset in a divorce. For vehicle insurance policies, find out whether your existing policy allows you to insure the vehicles you and your spouse drive if you are living separately and apart during a divorce. As I noted in chapter 3, you should review your existing and future insurance needs in contemplation of your divorce with an insurance professional.

2) Develop a plan.

As I have already stated, divorce causes change. Assets, debts, expenses and households are no longer shared by spouses when they divorce. Developing a plan that includes where you will live and how you will support yourself both in the early stages of divorce as well as the post-divorce stage is smart because it gives you direction as you go through the divorce process. You also need to know what to ask or negotiate for in terms of assets and support. Consider the circumstances of Genevieve, one of my former clients.

Genevieve was in her late forties when she was faced with a divorce. While she was college-educated, she had not worked in fifteen years. She had quit her job when the couple's first child was born, and her husband's income supported their family. They had been married for almost eighteen years. Although she was devastated and angry by all of the changes divorce would cause in her life, Genevieve sought advice from a financial advisor and me to develop a plan for herself both in the short term and in the long term. She did her own research on possible employment fields and education she would need to qualify for those fields. Genevieve carefully considered where she wanted to live with her two children and whether it was feasible for her to remain in the family home. Genevieve and her husband agreed to participate in mediation to resolve all issues for their divorce. Genevieve's planning and research were tremendously helpful to her in negotiating a settlement that took care of her needs in the immediate time frame, as well as in her future at and after retirement. She was confident in the planning she had done before mediation, and she knew what she needed from asset division and financial support to implement her plan.

I cannot stress enough the importance of having a plan or desired outcome when you divorce. As I have noted in previous chapters, the decisions made in your divorce will have a lifetime impact on you.

Know your financial needs in the present and future. Determine whether it makes sense financially to retain your home or purchase one after your divorce and know what you will need financially to do so. Often clients who have been out of the workforce for some time ask me if they need to find a job now that they are getting a divorce. They wonder if they won't receive as much or any spousal support or alimony if they are employed. Because laws related to spousal support and alimony are different among states, I cannot provide a definitive answer to these questions in this book. You should ask your own attorney this question. However, I do suggest that you consider what you would do for employment and what you would need with regard to education or training after your divorce to obtain employment if you are physically and emotionally healthy, and if you have several years or more ahead of you before retirement and you do not have sufficient assets or wealth available to you to consider early retirement.

3) Get real.

Very rarely in or after a divorce do the spouses get to live and spend their money exactly the way they did while they were married. Lifestyles commonly change because of a divorce. It's important to accept this reality. Know that you may have to adjust your monthly household expenses and expectations. If you have provided the primary financial support for your family throughout the marriage, acknowledge that you will have support obligations to your spouse both during and after divorce. Be realistic. If your spouse hasn't worked in years, expecting that he or she will become instantaneously employed at a prevailing wage just because you want a divorce is not realistic. Accepting this reality will help you develop a plan for managing your support obligations and securing your own financial future. Consult with an attorney and/or financial advisor to help you navigate the possible support obligation scenarios and asset division scenarios.

4) Try your best to be a responsible co-parent.

If you have children, know that divorce has a lifetime impact on them, too, beginning with the divorce process itself. Be mindful that the behavior that you and your spouse exhibit during a divorce affects your children. If you haven't separated yet or told your children that you plan to divorce, tap in to a resource to find out how to share the news with them. You and your spouse may want to share your decision to separate and divorce with your children together if that is an option. Consult with a mental health professional beforehand. Obtain guidance on how and what to tell your children. Seek advice on how to answer your children's questions about your divorce in a responsible and reassuring manner. Start reading a book about co-parenting or the impact of divorce on children so that you are knowledgeable about the emotional needs or struggles of your children and how you can support them.

5) Tend to your stress and emotions.

Divorce is stressful. Going through a divorce can make you feel like you are on an emotional roller coaster. Do not minimize or ignore your feelings or your stress. You cannot be helpful to yourself or your children if your stress levels and emotional state have erupted. Review chapter 2 again. Consider the suggestions I share in chapter 6.

6) Read relevant sources about divorce and your situation.

Thousands upon thousands of books and articles about divorce, parenting, and money management are available to help. Find a resource that resonates with you and heed the information. The following books are not an exclusive list by any means, but they include some good information that you should consider:

For increasing your understanding of finances:

Get Money Smart: Simple Lessons to Kickstart Your Financial Confidence & Grow Wealth, by Robert Pagliarini

Dave Ramsey's Complete Guide to Money, by Dave Ramsey

Start Late, Finish Rich: A No-Fail Plan for Achieving Financial Freedom at Any Age, by David Bach

For education on co-parenting, raising children during and after divorce:

The Co-Parents' Handbook, by Karen Bonnell, ARNP and MS, with Kristin Little, MA, MS, and LMCH

The Co-Parenting Survival Guide, by Elizabeth S. Thayer, Ph.D., and Jeffrey Zimmerman, Ph.D.

We're Still Family, by Connie Ahrons, Ph.D.

The Good Divorce, by Connie Ahrons, Ph.D.

Divorce Book for Parents, by Vicki Lansky

Bits of Wisdom

1. Avoid making uninformed or premature decisions during the divorce process.

2. Take time to prepare and become familiar with your current financial situation including monthly expenses, assets, debts and insurance policies.

3. Read articles or books about divorce and money management.

4. Develop a short-term and long-term plan for yourself.

5. Be realistic and accept that adjustments to lifestyle and spending commonly occur during and after a divorce.

6. Divorce has a lifetime impact on children.

7. Find resources to help you be an effective parent through the divorce and recognize that the behavior you and your spouse exhibit affects your children.

Chapter 5

Weigh Your Options

Many of us have heard stories about divorces where people behave badly and use their lawyers and the court system to perpetuate the conflict and unhappiness between them. Unfortunately, I've had cases in my career as a divorce lawyer where bad behavior has occurred. I once had a client who was so irritated that she had to live with her spouse in the family home temporarily that she did all sorts of things to make his life miserable, including tampering with his expensive eye cream, causing him painful and visibly noticeable reactions in his eyes. I have represented clients so desperate to claim their place as the children's primary caretaker that they have raced to pick up their kids from school before their spouse, needled their spouse out of chaperoning field trips, and concocted health-care issues just to be the parent who took the child to the doctor. I've also had cases where fighting over how to divide household possessions cost the parties in lawyer fees three times what the possessions were worth.

Fighting over possessions is only one battle in divorce litigation. The entire war with both parties represented by legal counsel can cost tens of thousands of dollars, if not more. I am not kidding. A handful of my cases have crossed over the $100,000 mark, with the divorce process lasting close to three years before a judge made the final determinations. Not one client in that handful of cases told me that he or she was grateful for the litigation process.

Did you ever watch the 1989 movie *War of the Roses*? The film follows a wealthy couple with a seemingly perfect marriage. When their marriage falls apart, material possessions become the center of an outrageous divorce battle. The wife throws the husband out of their house, but he moves back in after he discovers a legal loophole permitting him to stay. A war ensues between the two spouses, in which they do anything and everything to spite and humiliate each other. Possessions and furnishings are destroyed. The spouses threaten and inflict physical harm on each other. At the end of the movie, the spouses are discovered hanging dangerously from an insecure chandelier in their home, which subsequently plummets, and they both crash to their deaths on the floor below.

War of the Roses is a dark comedy. It came out before I went to law school, and I thought it was entertaining when I first watched it. When I watched it again years later, I was less entertained. Although the movie is fictional, the emotions felt by the feuding spouses and some of their behaviors are unfortunately very real for people going through divorce. Thankfully, the legal process in place to dissolve a marriage does not have to even faintly resemble this *War of the Roses*. You do not have to litigate. Litigation means that you and your spouse are using court intervention to resolve issues in dispute. In other words, when two parties cannot agree on certain matters, a judge decides. You do not need to allow a judge to control your fate, however, by making final decisions that will impact your life, your children's lives, and your family's future. You have other options.

Before hiring a lawyer or embarking on the legal process to dissolve your marriage, you should consider this question: "What do I want my divorce process to look like?" Really consider this question.

I would be very surprised if your answer is that you want to duke it out with your spouse in court, spend thousands upon thousands of dollars on attorneys' fees, lose your ability to make decisions for yourself, and feel taken advantage of at the end of the legal process. In my experience, most people who have used litigation to dissolve their marriage do not say that they appreciated the stressful, money-draining process that lasted so much longer than they had anticipated and that resulted in a less-than-satisfactory outcome for them. They do not feel satisfied by creating an even more strained relationship and increased bitterness (even outright hatred) between them and their spouse.

If you do not want an outrageous divorce war, how do you manage it? Several options are available to resolve your legal divorce that do not involve a court or judge calling the shots for you. These options can involve lawyers and other professional support in varying degrees. Here are the options:

- **DIY (Do It Yourself):** Some divorcing spouses are able to sit down together without lawyers, work through the details, and reach agreements on all issues related to their divorce. This option is extremely cost-effective as the spouses aren't paying lawyers' fees. If you can DIY your divorce, that is fantastic, but you should recognize that this is a legal process with certain legally binding documents that you will need to complete in the correct way. Even if you believe you have the easiest divorce in the world, I still highly encourage you to consult with a lawyer *before* any agreement is reached or documents are filed with the court to ensure that your interests are protected and you are not overlooking any detail that could come back to haunt you later.

- **Mediation:** Mediation is a process in which an impartial third party (i.e., the mediator) facilitates communication and negotiation between spouses with the goal of helping them reach a voluntary agreement. Mediation allows spouses to discuss their needs and interests and generate options for meeting those needs and interests to arrive at reasonable solutions. Mediation works well for spouses without power struggles in their relationship, although skilled mediators should be able to neutralize and/or assist with power imbalances that may infiltrate a mediation session. Attorney involvement in the mediation process also may help with power imbalances. However, divorcing spouses can participate in mediation without attorneys present. Mediation often reduces conflict, provides spouses with control over their divorce process and outcome, expedites a settlement, and tempers attorney fees.

- **Collaborative Divorce:** A Collaborative Divorce is a structured, voluntary dispute-resolution process where the spouses agree not to use litigation as a means of resolving their divorce. The spouses maintain decision-making control while receiving support and guidance from their respective attorneys in the process, as well as from other professionals such as divorce coaches, child specialists, or financial specialists. Transparency and privacy are key elements in a Collaborative Divorce.

- **Negotiation by Attorneys:** Negotiation by attorneys means that the divorcing spouses allow their respective attorneys to negotiate all disputes and reach a settlement. The negotiation may be done via written correspondence and/or a meeting between the attorneys. The spouses may be present for the meeting between their attorneys. While this approach is less adversarial and often more collegial, no third party is facilitating discussion, identifying needs or interests, and helping the parties generate or maximize options for their circumstances. Negotiation by attorneys often is done from the lens of the court—considering what a judge would do.

- **Hybrids:** A non-litigated divorce may use more than one of the above options. For example, spouses may attempt to DIY but then use mediation to resolve any thorny issues in their divorce. Spouses also may decide to proceed with a Collaborative Divorce after initially trying to talk with each other about their divorce. Spouses may start off with negotiation by attorneys and then engage a mediator if progress is not evident in the negotiations by or with their attorneys. Alternatively, spouses may use mediation to resolve most of their disputed issues and then turn over the final details to their attorneys to work through outside of mediation.

I have litigated many divorce cases. I also have mediated divorce cases, negotiated settlements outside of court, and represented clients in the Collaborative Divorce process. Hands down, I have learned that the path not litigated is almost always the better path. Sometimes litigation may be necessary, particularly when, despite best efforts, the other party won't come to the negotiation table. Not litigating your divorce does not mean that the process is all rainbows and unicorns, however. It cannot be easy—because divorce is always hard. However, I strongly believe that the options described above are better for divorcing spouses and their families. In my professional experience, people who choose not to litigate their divorce are faster to heal their emotions, move forward in their lives and transition from divorce.

Bits of Wisdom

1. The divorce process does not have to be a contentious or costly war.

2. Consider what you want your divorce process to look like before hiring an attorney.

3. Options are available to resolve your legal divorce that are more private, less stressful and not reliant on a judge making all necessary and important decisions for you.

Chapter 6

Take Care of You

Divorce may be the most traumatic life event you will experience. No matter what the reason or cause for the divorce or who initiated the process, separation and divorce are difficult and stressful. You should accept that your level of happiness may be shaken temporarily and that you may not function optimally at times. This is totally okay and normal. What is important here is that you address your own needs and receive support. Despite the emotional storm divorce brings, you still need to manage daily life, take care of your children if you have them, and participate in the process of dissolving your marriage, even if you do not want to be divorced.

Here are some strategies for coping with separation and divorce:

- **Tend to your emotions.** Take care of and responsibility for your own emotional well-being during this time. Accept that you may experience all sorts of intense emotions. Seek support from friends, family members, therapy, or a support group. Isolating yourself or burying your emotions can increase your stress and anxiety. Talking through what you are experiencing can make it less scary.

- **Your body is still a temple.** Be good to your body. Make the time to exercise, relax, and receive nourishment. Regular exercise relieves stress and helps improve your mood. Be mindful of how and what you are eating. A gallon of ice cream or a bag of potato chips may seem like a quick pick-me-up fix for sorrow and stress, but it does not have any positive long-term rewards for you. Food shouldn't be a source of continual comfort. Similarly, while a glass or two of wine can take the edge off, don't rely on alcohol as a coping strategy. Drugs also are a no-no. People often use food, alcohol, or drugs to numb themselves from painful emotions and stress. Overeating or drinking too much doesn't solve your problems. Your divorce is still part of your life after you've wolfed down the family-size bag of Cheetos or polished off the bottle of wine. Again, be mindful. Talk to your physician about an appropriate calming medication for a short period of time if you feel like the stress and emotions are too much for you.

- **You do not need to leap tall buildings in a single bound.** No one is Superman. Cut yourself some slack during this tough time. A divorce and separation can shake up you and your entire life. You may not be able to manage everything in your life, work, or home life at your usual, full capacity. It's okay. Figure out what "enough" looks like, instead of "all" or "everything." Focus on just doing enough for the time being.

- **Practice self-compassion.** Divorce happens. You are not a failure. Resist self-blame and self-criticism. Have compassion for yourself. Find ways to nurture yourself—hot baths, walks outside, reading, outings with friends, a massage, etc. Be kind and supportive of yourself, just as you would be for a good friend going through a divorce.

- **You cannot control everything. Really.** You cannot control your spouse. You cannot control how or what your spouse is feeling, saying, or doing as you go through a divorce. You may not be able to control the outcome or how long it will take to get through the process. But you can control and be responsible for your own behavior. You can control things such as what you have for lunch or when you exercise or go to sleep. Stay focused on what you can control and try to let go of the rest.

- **Maybe now is not the time to make a big decision.** Thinking logically can be a challenge during times of high stress and emotion. Divorce is one of those times, and you may feel like you need to make a lot of decisions as a result. However, you may want to delay making any big decisions until you feel like you can be rational and consider all options or consequences that may be associated with a specific decision. Putting off big decisions could be hard, because we tend to feel more in control when we make them. Practice patience and give yourself time.

- **Fun is advisable. Laughter is a must.** While you may not feel like having fun or laughing, you really should do both. Recreation, enjoying an activity, or spending time with a good friend is like medicine. You need fun and laughter in your life, and you need it even more when life doesn't seem so good. Sign up for the painting class you've wanted to take. Accept an invitation from a friend for coffee or lunch. Release the belly laughter each time an opportunity presents itself. The tough divorce stuff likely won't feel so gloomy or isolating if you make time for fun and laughter.

- **Create an amazing playlist and listen to the songs often.** You know how you feel when a favorite song comes on the radio. Music has a way of elevating the spirit and causing your lips to smile and your voice to sing. No doubt your spirit needs to be lifted at times when you go through a divorce. Build a playlist of songs that make you feel happy, inspired, or invincible. If you don't know where to start, Google "songs about overcoming adversity and challenges." Listen to the playlist in the car, while you exercise, or whenever you feel like you need to be lifted up in some way.

- **Take a social media break.** Social media is great. You can connect with friends and family members, share pictures and experiences, and learn a lot about other people you know. Yet seeing all the awesome things other people are doing when you aren't feeling at your best can bring you down further. If social media depresses you, take a little break from it. Also, be careful about sharing and posting on social media when you are going through a divorce. The picture you posted when you were out with your best gal pals with a margarita in your hand could turn up in court with an allegation that you have been partying hard and neglecting your kids. Similarly, the post you made when you were having a bad day and openly expressing feelings of discontent and discouragement may invite allegations of emotional instability. You may regret posting pictures from your Caribbean cruise, new car, or night out on the town if you have been telling your spouse or the court that you can't pay support because money is tight. You also may not want your spouse to see posts or pictures of you with your new paramour the day or two before you begin negotiating a settlement, as emotions could be stirred unfavorably and sabotage the settlement process. Be smart with social media. Resist the urge to post every little detail about your life.

- **Never underestimate the power of a good night's sleep.** Everyone functions better when they are well rested, but it's easy to minimize the importance of sleep when we are feeling stressed out or consumed by worry. Make sleep a priority for yourself as you are going through your divorce. Adequate rest helps you think clearly, manage daily tasks better, and respond to issues and scenarios that come up. If you are having trouble with sleep or your mind is spinning at night when you should be sleeping, try an herbal application like chamomile tea, or consider talking with your doctor about a temporary sleep aid.

- **Meditate or journal.** Reigning in all the feelings of uncertainty, upset, and disappointment can be overwhelming when you are going through a divorce. To temper these feelings, practice meditation or keep a journal. Meditation may sound too "new age" for you, but it simply is the practice of quiet thought with a purpose of greater awareness. How you meditate is completely up to you. Perhaps you have a mantra that you repeat when you meditate that helps give you strength. Maybe it's a poem. Many apps offer guided meditation exercises, including some that are designed specifically to help promote relaxation before bedtime. Journaling is another way to process all the thoughts and feelings swimming around in your head. No matter how jumbled, negative, or critical those thoughts and feelings may be, get them down on paper. By writing out your feelings or worries, you may gain a better perspective on your situation, or you may be able to distance yourself from some of the intensity of the emotion.

- **Wisely choose your friends.** No question, you need support from friends and family members when you are going through a divorce. Make certain, though, that the people whom you choose to hang out with during this difficult time are truly helpful to and supportive of you. Those friends with the best of intentions may not be best for you if they are droning on and on about their own divorce experience or repeatedly bashing your soon-to-be ex-spouse. Someone else's divorce experience is not your experience. Divorces are not one-size-fits-all. Repeatedly criticizing your spouse is not time well spent. Your friend's disaster of a divorce or a judge whom he or she thinks was so unfair is likely different from your situation. Also, the huge financial "win" another friend received from divorce court has nothing to do with you and your circumstances. Leave the legal analysis to your attorney. Spend time with people you enjoy, who bring you comfort, who help you keep your chin up, and who serve as a sounding board for you.

- **Being positive is powerful.** Being positive is hard when you are experiencing something that feels so negative. Do it anyway. Your mind and body benefit from your ability to be positive. Check out these facts:

  1) The average American spends 75 to 80 percent of the day complaining.
  2) Five minutes of complaining disrupts your immune system for four hours. Physical reactions include an increase in muscle tension and an adverse impact to blood flow.
  3) Even two minutes of talking positively and being appreciative after a complaining episode assists in counteracting the disruption to your immune system.[2]

---

2 Lecture by Dr. Fred Luskin, Stanford University, at the International Academy of Collaborative Professionals annual conference in October 2016.

- **Let your kids be kids and you be the grown-up, even if they are grown-ups.** Do not share your personal concerns and divorce details with your children. Too often adults feel an obligation to be open and transparent with their children about their divorce. The related emotions are too much for young children to manage, however. Adult children can become conflicted in their own feelings about their parents when one parent shares potentially negative or hurtful information about the other. What young children need to know about their parents' divorce is simple—they are loved, and they will have someone to care for them no matter what happens. For adult children, the message is not that much different. Adult children also need to know that they are loved. All children need to feel that they are not being asked to choose between their parents. Children should not have to decide where they should live, who should accompany them to school or sporting events, and where they should spend the holidays. Being a parent in a divorce situation regardless of your child's age still means that you place their needs above your own. Do not put them at the center of conflict with their other parent.

Yes, you may feel sad about not spending Thanksgiving with your children, but if you avoid a fight with the other parent, that is what's best for your children and your relationship with them. By reinforcing your love for your children and gratitude for time spent with them, even if not on a specific holiday, you demonstrate unconditional love and model compassion and resilience. Your children then know they can rely on your support, and they will reciprocate gratitude for the time spent with you without pressure or conflict.

Bits of Wisdom

1. Feeling less happy or less able to function during the divorce process is normal.

2. You need to manage daily life, take care of your children if you have them, and participate in the divorce process even if you do not want to be divorced.

3. Find support for yourself and implement strategies to help you cope with your emotions and the stress of a divorce.

Chapter 7

Move Forward

Life goes on after a divorce. Don't miss out on life because you are wallowing in unproductive feelings or self-doubt. You deserve better. Take the time you need to emotionally heal from the divorce. Don't impose a set time frame on when you should be "over" your divorce. If you are still struggling with feelings of sadness or loss after the legal divorce process is complete, find support for yourself through a mental health professional or a support group. Although it is normal for a person going through a divorce to experience feelings of anger, fear, or sadness for a period of time, if the feelings continue for months or years after the separation or divorce has happened, you can't truly move forward in life.

Practice forgiveness. Forgive your former spouse for whatever transgressions you believe he or she did or the upset and disruption he or she may have caused to your life. Forgiving your former spouse does not mean forgetting what happened, but it does mean letting go of a lot of the negative energy surrounding the experiences and memories. Also, forgive yourself. Let go of the guilt, frustration, or anger you have held for your role in the divorce and its impact on your children or former spouse. You need to live your own life and carrying the emotional weight of guilt or anger is an impediment to doing so. Forgiveness is huge and hard because it challenges our ego; sometimes we have an overwhelming need to feel like we are right. Forgiveness is not about being right, but more about garnering peace and traversing a path forward.

Remember that you control your own behavior. How you react and respond to your former spouse and situations that may arise in the future is all on you. Resist the impulse to engage in conflict or inflammatory communication, especially where your children are concerned. Respectful interaction with your former spouse is important if you have young children, but it is also relevant for grown children.

Rely on your team. If you haven't assembled a team as I suggested in chapter 3, take the time to do so now. The players on your team may vary depending upon your circumstances, but you at least should have a lineup ready to go. Get emotional support from a therapist if needed. Find an accountant to help you navigate tax issues or prepare your individual income tax return post-divorce. Use a financial advisor for assistance in developing your financial plan even if you do not believe that you have much in the way of assets. You do have a future ahead of you, and planning for that future can only benefit you. Start somewhere and have a financial advisor help you.

Make a will or change your will. If you and your former spouse prepared wills while you were married, you should change it after a divorce. If you don't have a will, you probably should create one. A will becomes effective after you have died; it designates a certain person to handle your affairs (i.e., an executor or personal representative) and sets forth how you want your property to be distributed. If you have a will that lists your former spouse as the executor or sole heir, you may want it to be changed. While some states have enacted statutes that automatically revoke provisions pertaining to a former spouse upon divorce, do not rely on these laws. The best course of action is to prepare a new will consistent with your actual intentions going forward. Your loved ones may appreciate having a road map on what you want to happen after you die. You may think you have plenty of time to have a will prepared, but everyone dies, and you should not procrastinate in the completion of this task.

Get a power of attorney. Unlike a will, a power of attorney becomes effective while you are alive, if you are unable to manage your affairs or make decisions for yourself. An unforeseen accident, head injury, or dementia, for example, can derail your life plans, and you must be ready if something bad happens. Now that you are newly single, you probably should have a trusted person designated to step into your shoes and act on your behalf should the need arise. If you have consulted with an attorney about preparing a new will, have the attorney prepare a power of attorney for you, as well.

Update your insurance policies and beneficiary designations. You may have designated your former spouse as the beneficiary or pay-on-death designee for a life insurance policy, bank account, or retirement account. You need to change each beneficiary designation you have in place after you are divorced. Do not overlook a beneficiary designation or pay-on-death designee on your checking or savings account. Often these designations are put in place when you establish the account, and you may not even remember that you did so. Assets with beneficiary designations in place pass outside of a will. This means that the financial institution is obligated to distribute the life insurance proceeds, funds on deposit, or retirement assets to the designated beneficiary, even if the will states something else. Prepare a new will and update your beneficiary designations so that your intentions for the distribution of your assets upon your death are clear and able to be carried out successfully.

Organize important documents, and make sure a trusted person knows where to find them. Do not make this a scavenger hunt. When emergencies or urgencies arise, delay and confusion in locating information will not benefit you. Help yourself by making sure a trusted person knows exactly where to find relevant information and documentation about you if an emergency occurs. Give the trusted person the business card or contact information for the attorney who assisted you in preparing a will or power of attorney. Tell the trusted person where to find the combination to your safe at home or the specific desk drawer where copies of your insurance policies are located.

Bits of Wisdom

1. Life happens after divorce. Don't miss out.

2. Seek professional help if you continue to struggle with feelings of anger, sadness or despair months after your divorce is final.

3. Plan for your future. Organize important documents. Assemble your team as described in chapter 3.

4. Review and change the beneficiary designations on all life insurance policies, retirement accounts and financial accounts.

5. Update or prepare a will and power of attorney.

Chapter 8

Learn from Others

I have attempted to share in this book what I believe are helpful insights and smart suggestions based on my experiences and observations as a divorce attorney for more than twenty years. I've represented and consulted with thousands of people throughout my career. These people have relied on me for guidance in incredibly personal matters, which makes me feel so grateful. As part of my process for writing this book, I contacted former clients and asked for assistance in responding to three questions. I was moved by how much clients wanted to share their own divorce experience to help others. I have included the responses below, and I am very appreciative to the clients who took the time to respond.

1. What advice or information was given to you while you were going through your divorce that was particularly helpful to you, whether that advice was from a professional, friend, family member, or someone else?

Don't waste time fighting over possessions; you'll pay two to three times more than what they are worth in attorneys' fees.

As much as possible, treat the divorce process as a business transaction; try to put your emotions behind you; if you can't, find someone who can give you rational advice throughout the process.

Try to get a clear understanding of the total divorce process with key events along the way like going to court and preparing for court.

Don't make any large purchases or consider any big financial decisions during this time because everything will be examined and potentially used against you.

Keep the goal in mind that you want to be friends with your spouse when the divorce is over; if you keep this mind-set, you might not be enemies by default.

Do not put your kids in the middle no matter what (even if that means deferring to the other parent to minimize the negative impact on your kids—whether they are adult children or young kids; it relieves so much pressure on them).

* * *

During the onset of my divorce process, I received helpful advice from the people on whom I leaned. My network of friends and family members consoled me and said that one day I would get through the pain. On an emotional level, I was advised to take life one day at a time. On a practical level, I was advised to make an action plan and seek legal counsel. During such an emotionally charged time, it was difficult for me to see a clear picture of my future needs, so I consulted a professional. Once I had obtained legal counsel, I was encouraged to strive for an amicable divorce, but I was also told that my first priority was making decisions that reflect the best interests of my children and myself. Additionally, I was advised to collect financial documentation so that I could propose a fair and reasonable division of property. I learned that there needed to be a business side to the divorce process. Other helpful advice given to me was to be factual and direct on the court documents and to be respectful during the court proceedings.

* * *

Have patience in the process, even though human nature pushes us to get through it as fast as possible. Good things come from the time it takes to go through the process with patience. It helps with making sure that decisions are as thoughtful and clear as they can be. Letting it take six months or a year isn't a bad thing, because it allows time to resolve pieces that are difficult with solutions that you can live with long-term. Do not rush.

If you have children and a significant financial estate, break the process into two pieces and keep them separate. Don't let the emotions surrounding one dictate your efforts on the other. One is personal and the other is business.

Listen to the advice of others, but at the end of the day, make sure all your decisions are ones you can live with.

Find one or two people whom you can discuss the details with, people who listen and help you see all sides.

No one wins in divorce. Don't look at it like winning and losing. The process is a constant negotiation for everyone's best guess on what is fair.

Hire an attorney who matches your character, but also whom you know has the strength and endurance to fight for you if necessary.

* * *

Be clear about what you want. Prioritize your needs/wants. Tell your attorney these things. Think about what motivates the person you are divorcing. Tell your attorney that information as well.

* * *

When I was initially going through mediation, I was eager to be amenable and agree with what my ex-husband proposed without really considering all the facts or consequences. I just wanted to get the divorce over with and did not want any ill will between us. My divorce attorney helped me to slow down and really look at the facts and history of the purchase of our home. I had used my inheritance to pay off the mortgage, but I had thought that our home was community property [marital property] and that I would not be able to recoup my inheritance. Until I talked through this issue with my divorce attorney,

I did not know that I could, indeed, request my inheritance funds back before the equity in the home was divided. In general, the legal counsel I received was to thoroughly review every detail of each mediation session, go over my records, and hold my own. I went through three mediation sessions on my own and consulted with my divorce attorney before and after each session. I was better equipped each session with the facts and more confident to state what I thought was equitable and fair. It was invaluable to have my divorce attorney "on call" literally by phone to ask questions throughout the mediation process. She asked important questions and had knowledge of the law and the divorce process that I was completely unaware of at the onset. What helped me also was that my divorce attorney let me know what I could do on my own to keep the overall costs down. The attorney fees for my divorce were much less as a result.

* * *

When I was going through my divorce, I had two advocates—my divorce attorney and my therapist, who was a licensed clinical social worker. Having strong advocates helped me navigate the legal and emotional morass of divorce. I felt I had someone who believed in me during my lowest points. Divorce is so hard. Having a team of advocates is essential to walking through it. My court declarations were very well written and accurately reflected my story. I was fortunate to have an attorney who demonstrated self-respect, expressed client respect, earned the court's respect, and possessed community respect. The best advice I got was to remove my son from my ex-spouse's house and the toxic environment caused by his stepmother and maintain primary custodial status.

* * *

The best advice I received was to get a good lawyer. You may need your lawyer for many years. Get referrals for attorneys from friends.

I tell all my friends who are going through a divorce to make sure and get everything in the parenting plan. Details are important. Also, you may think it will be amicable in the beginning, but be wise and protect yourself, your assets, and your children. You never know how your ex-spouse will act as time goes on.

* * *

Take the time needed to make this important decision and seek support from those who know you and love you. I sought therapy, too. It was invaluable to help me sort through my own head and heart and to learn that I would not necessarily feel good about the divorce until it was over. Then the healing begins.

Find an attorney who will work with you and be your truthful and realistic advocate. My attorney was a great advocate for me during the process. Find an attorney who is sensitive enough to know you and your situation. You want an attorney with a personal approach but who is direct enough to push a bit when the situation calls for it and to hold back when it's a wise move. A good attorney knows the next steps and how to take them without railroading you into them. I needed someone who could help me weigh various options and help me find the one that was best for me.

Take care of yourself in this difficult process. Whatever self-care looks like for you, do that. A lot.

* * *

The court system and the divorce will not give you emotional justice. You will lose friends, in-laws, and even family members in the process. This is okay. You will be surprised as to who will end up being there for you. Find a good support group. Find a lawyer whom you trust and who is an advocate. Don't be afraid to change attorneys if it isn't a right fit.

Consider talking to a child psychologist to learn how to transition to a new normal for all members of the family.

Remember who you are and play the long game. Take your time when making decisions.

Don't rush the healing process. You will survive this and even thrive. It is a chapter in your life, not the whole book. Take care of yourself – mentally, physically, spiritually, and emotionally.

Your kids will be okay.

* * *

Find an attorney whom you trust and connect with and talk to that attorney first. Get the lay of the land (i.e., the divorce process) and know what options you have before making any decisions or telling anyone your intentions. Take care of yourself first.

* * *

The advice to live in different rooms while sorting out the process of the divorce was good advice. Having one of the partners move out of the house before the parenting plan is finalized sets a precedent for the children.

One of the best things that we did was to designate a certain percentage of our assets for paying for the kids' future college expenses. This avoided either of us taking cash from the sale of real estate and using it for our own purposes.

Working with a mediator to develop our divorce plan was the best step we took. We drew up the specifics of our plan with the mediator, who helped us understand the different issues and categories to work through.

Considering different potential life changes which can/will happen after divorce is likely a good idea. For example, how will each parent contribute to college? What if either parent moves to a new location?

Support from my friends was invaluable. It was a very tough emotional time. To be at odds with my former spouse was a very difficult experience.

It was toxic to spend too much time around other divorced men and women who were bitter about their experience and who spent too much talking about the unfairness of the laws for their situation. In the end, we all need to pick ourselves up and move on with life.

* * *

Believe it or not, the most helpful advice I received was from my divorce attorney. People had been trying to tell me for years about my ex-husband. It wasn't until through my divorce attorney (someone I did not know) that I accepted what I was told— that this man was a bully. I felt so scared, and this made complete sense. Knowing I had my divorce attorney on my side and that I could lean on her to provide strength and insight where I had none was the most helpful thing during this time.

I tried to always be respectful of my divorce attorney's time and never ask questions that I couldn't figure out on my own. Just knowing I had support in case I needed it was the most comforting thing. My divorce attorney was a strong woman whom I could build my own strength through and who could be a voice for me when I felt at the time I had none.

* * *

I would say that disclosing everything with your attorney and asking for advice and guidance along the way is key. Stay patient and rely on your attorney to assist you in making rational decisions rather than emotional ones.

* * *

A helpful piece of advice that I was given when I knew that my marriage was not able to be fixed was to get legal advice before making any big decisions that would have an impact on my son and me.

* * *

The first thing that I was told was to get a good lawyer and to keep records of all communication. I was also told to communicate with my spouse only through my lawyer, which helped me a lot during a difficult time.

* * *

I had a wise friend tell me to make a list of pros and cons about my marriage and then to look and decide about leaving or staying. The best thing I did for myself was leave that marriage. I am just now, after two years, starting to find myself as a good person and truly loving my life for the first time.

2. Looking back at the time in which you were going through your divorce, what would you have preferred to know that you did not?

The power of seeking and trying to get the divorce case resolved through mediation early on to prevent having things drag on and then go to court. I would have liked to have known how to better prepare for court even though it was a year out.

I should have sought more information about the divorce process.

It was often unclear to me what the next step was and what we were waiting for. I would have liked to know the necessary steps to get to final resolution sooner and how to expedite those steps.

* * *

I feel as if I was well informed. At the time of my divorce, I was advised to be more specific on the holiday schedule in my parenting plan. My original plan was obscure. I assumed my ex-husband and I could have a working co-parenting relationship. However, this was/is not the case. Ultimately, we needed to mediate [after our divorce was final] to have our parenting plan clarified. The parenting plan is like a Bible, and the mediated version is followed religiously. I have learned that the parenting plan is vital.

* * *

Do as much of the thinking as you can on your own. Get legal advice and general recommendations and then think them over. The more decisions you make for yourself will help in the healing and bring more peace when it is over. This takes a lot of strength, maturity, and personal grace—but it is worth it. You won't look back and say, "My attorney did a poor job." You will be more content with your new life if you hold each piece of the divorce process and don't leave the decisions to others. Sometimes I wanted someone else to do the work for me—but in the end, I'm glad I did all that I could.

* * *

*I feel that I was adequately informed through all stages of the divorce process. I can't think of anything that I did not know. As a professional, my divorce attorney communicated well with me and provided good legal counsel to me. Being my advocate, she also knew how to communicate with opposing counsel. Additionally, out compassion and wisdom, my divorce attorney knew that it was healthy for me **not** to entirely know the content of* *the blizzard of communications coming from my spouse's attorney.*

* * *

I did not really understand all of the costs involved. Many people think that if the other side wants to argue and carry on, the expense should be on them, but it is not. For example, if your spouse has lost/ fired their lawyer and wants to continue to argue with your lawyer, you will pay for the time.

I incurred a lot of fees with my first attorney on the discovery process. It was not clear to me that I needed every month of everything [documents], and I was charged a lot for the legal assistant to gather what I was missing. I could have retrieved them myself had I known. I still do not understand why I had to do discovery, or why only I had to do it for both my spouse and me at my expense.

* * *

I don't think I needed more information at the start. I got some basic parameters of time and money from my attorney, and the rest unfolded as it needed to. It was a bit more expensive than I had hoped, but that was because of feet-dragging on the part of my now-ex-spouse. My attorney helped me decide how to push through and get movement, but those actions cost more time and money. This was a necessary part of the process, and I don't regret it.

I was surprised at how the issues with my now-ex that led me to divorce continued to play out during the process—for both of us.

* * *

[During the divorce] I didn't fully understand how difficult it would be to modify a parenting plan later on.

I didn't realize how much I still would have to deal with my ex after the divorce was finalized because of co-parenting.

* * *

I did not understand how long it [the divorce process] could take and that it's not about what's fair.

* * *

I wish I had known that all of my retirement could be split, including the portion I had accumulated before we married.

I would caution people in new relationships when there is a significant difference in earning potential and contribution to the family finances. This type of relationship can work, but it appears to be a relic from previous generations.

* * *

I had researched quite a bit up front, or at least as much as I could. The most helpful experience I had was the consultation with a divorce attorney to answer questions, learn possibilities, and talk about my situation.

* * *

I am not sure if there was anything I would have preferred to know. I asked a lot of questions regarding the time frame for the legal process, potential costs, and potential outcomes.

* * *

Looking back, I wish that I fully understood the financial side of the divorce better than I had at the time. I did not completely understand from my first attorney that signing a quit claim deed to our co-owned property did not mean that my ex-husband was under any legal obligation to refinance the property in his name only. My name was still on his mortgage for at least five years after our divorce was final, which impacted my ability to get a loan if I had needed one due to my debt-to-income level. I would have liked to have known that the agreement to refinance should have been specifically spelled out in the divorce agreement.

* * *

I wish I had known that it was so hard to prove what you owned before marriage although it was worth fighting for. I would say always keep good records of what you have or owned before you get married.

I wish I had understood more about how the court makes parenting plan decisions (even if you think it is not right). I would have liked to understand more about child support and how it was calculated.

3. Thinking back on your divorce experience, what would you do differently?

I would have retained a different attorney from the outset. I chose an attorney who was well-known in name rather than one who was better suited for my personality and needs and who was hands-on.

* * *

Thinking back on my divorce, I wish I could have been less emotional. I also wish I had known to explore the postsecondary education topic more. At the time of the divorce, I was advised to think about this and create a plan, but to me it all seemed so far away and I was not ready to think about it. Overall, I should have paid more attention to the details of my parenting plan, but I think my emotions got in the way.

* * *

I'm pleased to say that at the one-year mark I can still say, other than that I wish divorce did not exist, I have no regrets with the process. I would have trusted the process more, even though not one fiber of your being wants to trust anything during that time.

* * *

What would I do differently? Perhaps be a better negotiator? I just wanted out. That being said, my life is good now.

* * *

I can't think of anything that I would do differently. Why change winning? We were undefeated in all of our court appearances, numbering more than half a dozen. Things that worked for me when going through divorce included: being proactive with my self-care; getting massages, seeing a therapist, exercising, journaling, listening to music, and being creative (I wrote close to forty poems during and after my divorce). Well, since I am twice divorced, I did something differently that I should have done after my first divorce; this time I heeded the advice from Alanis Morissette's lyrics in the song "Moratorium," which I recommend to all who go through a divorce.

Don't jump into a new relationship or develop a new romantic interest. After divorce, get whole and healthy first without "the flavors of entanglement."

* * *

I would have not tried to settle as quickly (which did not turn out to be quickly after all). I retained much debt that was not mine. I gave up new furnishings and housewares. I also would have not let him pack while I was not there, as he took items that did not belong to him and half of sets of things.

I would have thought further into the future regarding the parenting plan. Our daughter was not in school, and school vacations played a lot into disagreements later when she was of school age.

What I did right was not give up on time with my daughter. I fought to have her with me the majority of the time and any amount of money is worth this.

* * *

My initial answer to this question was to move faster to file [the divorce petition] and push a little harder to keep things moving, but that's only hindsight. In the thick of it, you don't have that vantage point. Keep in mind that this is YOUR divorce and you have to live with the process, timelines, and results. Seek advice and support, but ultimately you need to do your divorce process in your own way. That takes me back to the importance of a good attorney who will be your advocate when you can't see clearly and don't know all of the options.

* * *

A divorce is a difficult time, but it doesn't have to be damaging or venomous.

* * *

I shouldn't have given my ex the benefit of the doubt and set more specific parameters on my parenting plan.

I should have spent more time interviewing psychologists and found one who was right for my son early on in the divorce process.

I wouldn't be as fearful all the time.

* * *

I would have kept as much contact as possible through my attorney—to avoid potential bullying and scare tactics. It may not be the most cost-effective method, but it removes some of the animosity and stress.

* * *

We considered the case for us to stay together until after the kids left the house. This was listed as an option in a book. We ended up not doing this, but I know of a couple of other families that are making this option work. A downside of this is that it delays moving on and each partner becoming self-sufficient.

* * *

I really appreciated the direct, fair, and professional advice my attorney gave me. I certainly would not try to "go it alone." I think representing myself would have been a critical mistake.

* * *

If I were to do anything differently, I would have taken a trusted family member or friend to every appointment possible along with me. I would have had someone to be that second set of ears and a note taker for me. It was difficult to be composed and fully present [when meeting with my divorce attorney] while being subjected to written and verbal abuse from my soon-to-be ex-husband. I was extremely impacted emotionally during the divorce. In hindsight, I did not always have the full ability to hear what was being said during attorney meetings and to think clearly about decisions I was trying to make.

* * *

I would have only communicated through my divorce attorney. The process was painful, but she [my divorce attorney] made it less painful, and she fought for me and what was best for my child.

* * *

My divorce was a lot different from most because we had been married for thirty-one years. For me, I was very unhappy throughout my entire marriage. I hung in there thinking things would get better.

There was constant arguing and no respect. I wish I would have known that, if after numerous years of counseling and nothing is getting better, you should find the courage to divorce. I felt I was truly stuck in the marriage.

The legal and emotional parts of the divorce process are not the same for every person. The responses to the three questions above demonstrate the different experiences, feelings, and perspectives of people about their divorce. Your circumstances are unique to you. I hope that some of my former clients' responses resonate with you in some way. Most importantly, however, be wise in your use of the information and advice you obtain. You *can* get through this difficult time. Prepare for the unexpected as well as the expected and have compassion for yourself. I wish you all the best.

Acknowledgments

I am blessed with a close family and wonderful friends. I wasn't sure what would happen when I first started jotting down my ideas for this book, but I had support from the outset. For that encouragement, I am thankful.

My parents taught me the value of education and helped me develop common sense from an early age. Mom and Dad, I love you both.

Many training sessions and conferences have expanded my thinking and changed the way I practice law. I have a great deal of admiration for the professionals who have influenced my work, but none more so than Woody Mosten.

My colleagues in Collaborative Practice mentor and inspire me. I especially appreciate Nancy Retsinas for introducing me to the collaborative way and being a trusted colleague throughout my career.

If it were not for the BASH ladies, I might not have written this book. They are a blunt yet caring group of women who provide me with honesty, experience, and accountability. They were first to tell me to go for it.

My kids were excited to learn that their mom was writing a book and less so when I told them the topic. They make my life real and warm.

The words "thank you" are not adequate to express my gratitude for my husband, Tom Hagley Jr. He didn't run when I told him two weeks after we got married that I was quitting the law firm where I had worked for six years to start my own practice. He didn't get flustered when he would find books about divorce lying around our house, and he was incredibly supportive of my efforts to shape and transform my practice. Tom read and edited the first draft of this book and encouraged me to take the next step. He keeps me steady and fills my heart.

Note to the Reader

This book is intended to provide general information and should not be construed as legal or financial advice. Readers should not consider this book as a substitute for receiving advice from a lawyer, accountant, financial advisor, or mental health professional relevant to their specific circumstances or situation.

About the Author

Juliet Laycoe is the principal attorney at Juliet Laycoe PC, a Vancouver, Washington, law firm. She dedicates much of her practice to helping people through one of the most life-altering and traumatic events—divorce. Her twenty years of experience include representation of clients in complex divorce litigation, as well as in high-conflict custody disputes. Ms. Laycoe also is trained as a collaborative practitioner and mediator. She enjoys working with clients to resolve disputes outside of court through settlement, negotiation, mediation, or collaborative law.

Admitted to both the Washington State Bar and the Oregon State Bar, Ms. Laycoe has practiced law since 1998. She graduated from Pacific Lutheran University with a bachelor of arts degree in legal studies and sociology and Lewis & Clark Law School with a juris doctor. Her practice has emphasized family law, including divorce, guardianship, estate planning, and estate administration.

Ms. Laycoe is a member of various professional associations. She presents at continuing legal

Photo credit: Stephanie Gawley, Studio G Photography

education seminars and programs. She is active in and maintains memberships in collaborative professional groups, including Collaborative Professionals of Washington (CPW) and the International Academy of Collaborative Professionals (IACP).

Ms. Laycoe helped establish the George and Donald Simpson American Inn of Court in southwest Washington and previously served on the local county Superior Court Bench Bar Committee. She has volunteered in the community and has supported numerous causes and charitable organizations. She has been recognized with the following honors and awards:

Vancouver Rotary Club, Rotarian of the Year, 2010;

Clark County Bar Association, Ken Weber Community Service Award, 2003;

Vancouver Business Journal, Accomplished and Under 40 Award, 2002;

Vancouver Rotary Club, Rookie Rotarian of the Year, 2002; and

City of Vancouver and Vancouver National Historic Reserve Trust, General George C. Marshall Public Leadership Award, 2000.

Ms. Laycoe resides in southwest Washington with her husband and two children.

For more information, please visit
www.julietlaycoe.com
and
www.divorce-wisdom.com.

CPSIA information can be obtained
at www.ICGtesting.com
Printed in the USA
FFHW020142291218
50005217-54739FF